DOWNLOADING the UNIVERSE

CLICK HERE!

MIHOKO SEKIDO

SAKURA PUBLISHING
Hermitage, Pennsylvania
USA

DOWNLOADING

THE

UNIVERSE

CLICK HERE!

MIHOKO SEKIDO

DOWNLOADING THE UNIVERSE: CLICK HERE!

Copyright © 2014 by Mihoko Sekido

All rights reserved. Published in the United States by Sakura Publishing in 2014. No part of this publication may be reproduced, distributed, or transmitted in any form or by any means, including photocopying, recording, or other electronic or mechanical methods, without the prior written permission of the publisher, except in the case of brief quotations embodied in critical reviews and certain other noncommercial uses permitted by copyright law. For permission requests, write to the publisher, addressed "Attention: Permissions Coordinator," at the address below.

Sakura Publishing
PO BOX 1681
Hermitage, PA 16148
www.sakura -publishing.com

ORDERING INFORMATION:

Quantity sales, special discounts are available on quantity purchases by corporations, associations, and others. For details, contact the publisher at the address above. Orders by U.S. trade bookstores and wholesalers. Please contact Sakura Publishing:
Tel: (330) 360-5131; or visit
www.sakura-publishing.com.
Book Cover and Interior Design by Rania Meng
Edited by Derek Vasconi
Chief Editor: Peter Santilli

First Edition
Printed in the United States of America
ISBN-10: 0991180712
ISBN-13: 978-0-9911807-1-4
14 13 12 11 10 / 10 9 8 7 6 5 4 3 2 1

ACKNOWLEDGMENTS

I would like to thank my parents, who have been there for me throughout my most challenging times. Special thanks to my friend Jim who helped me to envision the direction of the book; Derek, my writing and editorial "coach;" and everyone else who helped and supported my endeavor for happiness at different stages of my life.

CONTENTS

Preface
A Little About Me

Chapter 1
{01}

happiness downloads

Chapter 2
{13}

relationship downloads

Chapter 3
{27}

health and beauty downloads

Chapter 4
{49}

love, romance, and sex downloads

Chapter 5
{65}

laws of the universe downloads

Chapter 6
{77}

manifesting abundance downloads

Conclusion
About the Author

I dedicate this book to my mother, Akiko Sekido.

She has always believed in me.

PREFACE

This book was born out of a wisdom that exists within the vast pool of knowledge in the Universe. I have been called upon to document anything and everything that came through me, since I am nothing but an ordinary person—like you.

This book is a tool, a guide, a coach; it is wisdom, encouragement, magic, a place to get inspiration, and a place to find solutions for life. However you would like to use this book is entirely up to you. It isn't written in any order of significance. You can start reading from any chapter or page as you wish. There are wide varieties of topics that are covered in this book. These include: health, beautification, love, romance, sex, happiness, the law of attraction, money and material abundance, career, and more.

This book is a documented collection of what I call "Universal Downloads." After I started to write, I wasn't certain whether or not to take credit for the information that came through me. Yet I am here to share the wisdom that I have received simply by living my life.

I have never formally studied philosophy or religion, but some of what you will see in this book may resemble particular philosophies or religions. That is because information exists in the vast pool of the Universal library, so to speak, and all of us are just borrowing the information and sharing from the same place. That is why, without me ever studying philosophy or religions, I might sound as if I actually have. This also means the "truth" that exists in this Universe is Universal, and it can come through me, or you, or anyone.

I also want to share some knowledge gained from life experiences and events. This isn't just about abstract concepts. I am going to show you how you can apply these "Universal Downloads" in your everyday life.

A LITTLE ABOUT ME

My name is Mihoko, and it's fair to call me an adventurous modern Japanese woman from Tokyo. I came to America in 1999 with a passport, $400 in my pocket, and a big dream. I wanted to be independent and live in America. So what did I do? I ran away from my somewhat modern yet still mostly traditional family in Japan to live and work in New York. Right after I arrived, I landed a big IT job and an attractive hipster, native New Yorker husband. Despite some drama I had created with my Japanese family, my dream seemed to have come true!

In reality, moving to New York was just the beginning. My life soon began to take many turns and surprising twists. I went through several high-stress corporate jobs. My marriage became unfulfilling. The money I was making didn't provide any sense of accomplishment. Eventually, I started to see the real bankruptcy deep within my soul. No matter how many nice dresses and shoes I possessed, I felt empty and unhappy!

So, after many, *many* twists and turns, including my marriage ending in divorce, becoming deathly ill, and temporarily moving back to Japan to recover, I came to a place of simple realization:

Happiness is fulfilling your soul's desire.

FROM NEW YORK TO SAN FRANCISCO

I moved to San Francisco in 2005 in hopes of getting away from the icy New York winters. I longed to enjoy a warmer climate. Well, I was off about 500 miles to the north. San Francisco had its share of frosty nights that reminded me of New York! At least I got myself a new boyfriend in the first two weeks after moving to San Francisco. And I let go of my material desires and possessions. I made a choice to lead a green-conscious, organic life.

I went from being a Shu-Uemura-green-eye-shadow-loving, Prada-stiletto-wearing fashionista to an organic-hemp-tee-shirt-wearing, bare-faced-new-age-raw-foodist (that is, someone who eats mainly un-cooked plant-based foods)! I underwent a total makeover. It made me feel happier and closer to my soul's desire.

Still, a nagging question kept haunting me:

What is my purpose in this life?

A RAW FOOD DIET AND THE AVATAR PHENOMENON

By the way, eating natural foods can help you "get connected" to the earth. One will experience something that I call "The Avatar Phenomenon". Similar to the thematic elements found in the movie *Avatar*, I experienced what is called "synchronicity," and began living in a reality where nothing is coincidence and everything happens for a reason. Things and events were happening in my life that let me see connections between everything around me. My intuition became sharper, and after many confirmations with real events, I started to trust more of my gut feelings and mysterious messages that appeared everywhere—on my computer screen, in digital numbers, words that entered my ears, emails, radio, billboards, people, nature, even words written on the jackets of people walking past me at the precise moment I would ask a question.

ACCELERATED MANIFESTATION OF THOUGHTS

After all this started to happen, I theorized that *all* things are possible to manifest in this dimension, as all existence in the Universe is energy and God, or the Creator. This is also the *Consciousness* that resides in all existence, including humans.

Suppose we are all God; then you could argue that we all have the innate power to effect any changes or creation from nothingness into existence. When I started to believe this, it seemed that the manifestation of my non-physical ideas and thoughts had sped up one hundred times faster than before! I was able to manifest my desires and ideas at light speed. For example, I would write down the exact conditions and features of the apartment in which I wished to live, down to the rent amount and move-in terms (such as no deposit, a nice vegetarian roommate, and preferably in North Beach, San Francisco), and I got this exactly as I had written! In fact, it seemed that whatever I would write down on a piece of paper with the intention of bringing it into reality manifested within a short period of time, sometimes within hours. *It happened.*

Sounds excellent, doesn't it? I, Mihoko, the great manifester, would have been able to realize all her hopes and dreams—right? Except there was one big problem. I didn't realize that I hadn't yet mastered the ability to tame the vicious, wild horse that was my mind. I began to manifest *all* my unconscious thoughts and feelings, both positive and negative. And when I had predominantly negative feelings, my life took a huge plunge into a downward spiral until I finally hit the very bottom.

GOING FROM "JUST FOOD" TO ADOPTING A SPIRITUAL APPROACH

In 2007, after experiencing a severe trauma that stemmed from domestic violence, my body started to fall apart at an alarming rate. Being an author of the first Japanese book on the raw food diet, *Hajimetemi-yo Raw Food Seikatsu*, I originally tried to heal myself with just raw foods, as I did to heal my facial eczema back in early 2000. After seeing that foods didn't help me at all, and that my body was still breaking down and looked like it aged about twenty years, I realized something very important about consciousness and energy:

All matter originates from energy.

From this point, I began to look *within,* to heal the root cause of the trauma I had experienced. I remembered the time I had visited a temple in Japan and had seen a statue of a Buddha deep in meditation. It is said that Buddha sat under a Linden tree for forty-nine days to achieve a sense of Nirvana. So I began to imitate the Buddha and practice what he did 2,500 years ago. I practiced various type of meditation and worked with holistic healers that appeared in my life.

I can heal, I said to myself. *I will not only heal, but will become a new and better person.*

DOWNLOADING FROM THE UNIVERSE

Soon afterwards, I started to get "information" from everywhere. Sometimes it was a suggestion, like *look here*, *go there*, *do this,* and so on. These thoughts guided me to the path of total healing, rejuvenation, and transformation. I began to call these spontaneous receipts of information "Universal Downloads".

It wasn't too long before my body healed and I felt more pleasant than ever. I became a changed person, like a Phoenix born rising from the ashes.

To everyone who reads this book: I am going to share these downloads with you. They changed me and made me who I am today, and it's my ardent hope that they can help you, too. Are you ready?

Then CLICK ON....

CHAPTER ONE

happiness downloads

Would you like to hear what you are here for? What your life purpose is?

PUT SIMPLY, IT'S TO BE HAPPY. I HAVE FIGURED OUT—FINALLY—THAT OUR LIFELONG PURPOSE IS *HAPPINESS*.

 This means living a soul-led life in every way, and to do this, you must first know yourself. This is why it has been so important that we experience life in its entirety, both the light and the dark, from every angle. Life has taught me that I am meant to attain oneness. To be one with the Universe means to be one with yourself, to be whole. There you will find that there are really no "angles" by which to approach life, but an entirety. This journey encompasses more than a lifetime; our lives are merely a preparation for a grander wholeness.

 In our uninformed efforts to be happy, content, and whole, we strive vaingloriously in this three-dimensional world. Day in and day out, we get up to go to work, to school, to take care of family, in hopes of acquiring contentment—to become whole. As these attempts so often seem to fall flat, we must ask ourselves: what does being "whole" mean? Are we missing something?

I came to realize that we human beings, whether consciously or unconsciously, aspire to grow in an ever-expanding manner, much like the universe from which we were born. The universe itself is continuously evolving; its intrinsic intelligence is perpetually growing more and more refined. So too do we humans, as components of the universe, become more refined in the process. After all, the universe consists of several different dimensions, and there's a great deal more to the world we live in than what can be seen with the naked eye.

We are the Universe, and the Universe is us.

DOWNLOAD

Our Universe is home to every conceivable mathematical law. For millennia, we humans have struggled to divine these universal laws; we call this study "science," and its application, "technology." Ours is a culture of advancement. How is it that the stuff of science fiction decades ago has today become reality? The answer is that our exploration of science reflects the unfolding universal intelligence within us all. It is an intelligence born into us from this Universe, an innate capacity to just "know" at the gut level. It provides us with the ability and drive to actualize inspiration and ideas into material reality. How we each manifest this depends on our individual life journeys.

You want to have that dream car, job, vacation, house, or lover because you want to
be happy.

You want to be healthy because you want to be happy; illness, as we all know, amounts to unhappiness. However, as an illness can also win us sympathy and showings of love, some of us allow the subconscious to make us sick.

Life is like a vast ocean with islands and dry land here and there. You can swim toward respite, or you can drown. If you wish to manifest a satisfying life, you must first learn to swim. Otherwise, you'll be forever in need of rescue from others as you gasp for air, unable to tread water. You will be grateful for such moments of relief, but soon you will realize that you will always be living life on someone else's terms. Those who know how to swim can command their own fates.

While you are swimming in this ocean, you might dream of an island on which you can build your material life. The number of possible islands you can dream up is infinite; you can craft whatever sort of fantastic island you please, but you must continue to swim. But if you've got no island ideal to consume your passions, you'll begin to feel lost—swimming will become tiresome, and you might find yourself drowning.

The direction in which you swim is almost irrelevant. Simply enjoy your watery voyage and let your mind play with hopeful notions of your dream island, and it is certain to appear. Do this with complete faith in your ability to manifest your dream, as doubt will leave you tethered to the sea. So learn to swim, enjoy the endeavor, and keep your mind focused on the joyful creation of your dream.

Lack of appreciation disconnects us from being whole, and this causes unhappiness. You must remain eternally optimistic, no matter what happens to you.

Deep down, I think have always known that the shortest path to happiness is to keep going, never minding when life challenges you with seemingly impossible situations that reek of negativity. As long as you keep moving with never-ending optimism, you can move mountains.

Nobel Prize-winning scientist Eiichi Negishi credited his "eternal optimism" for keeping him moving toward his eventual success. His words reached a huge amount of people around the world; to me, it confirmed my new way of thinking. And in terms of my religious leanings, I have long described myself as a follower of eternal optimism.

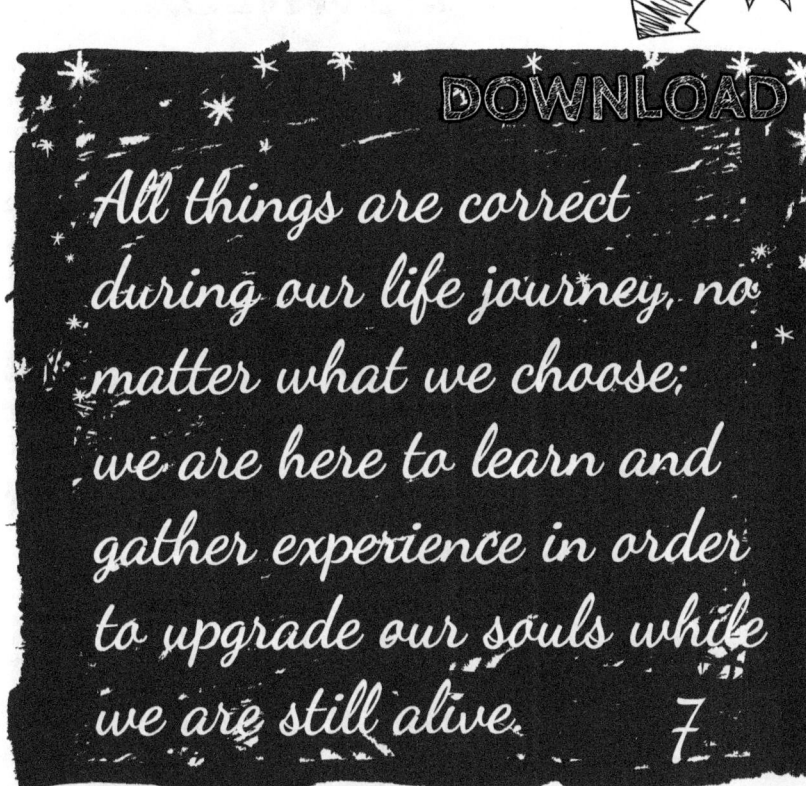

All things are correct during our life journey, no matter what we choose; we are here to learn and gather experience in order to upgrade our souls while we are still alive.

In a big picture sense, there are really no "good" or "bad" experiences; there are simply experiences that, regardless of how you describe them, still benefit the soul either way. You are here to collect memories, to remember that you are your destiny's master, and to be whole. You are your own Lord.

You might say to yourself, "I've been unhappy all of my life. Is it too late to start?" The answer is a resounding "no." Summon the wherewithal to start fresh, and begin your journey toward happiness now.

DOWNLOAD

I am nameless. I am without identity. I am free. This is a brand new moment. I can choose to be and do anything, right now. I can start fresh.

We've all seen the older people with hardened faces and deeply-etched vertical lines across their foreheads. They look angry, or as if they are in agony.

This is the physical manifestation of their minds, a result of thinking agonizing thoughts and feeling agonizing emotions. If you spend a lifetime beating yourself up, you will end up with the same sort of weathered countenance. Being at ease and possessing a mind at peace creates a peaceful face. The key to feeling peaceful is to practice compassion.

Being compassionate with others begins with compassion for yourself. Holding grudges against someone else only hurts you, not the other person. It hurts your body, as it is counter to our being, physically and spiritually, to do anything other than love. Love and compassion not only cultivate happiness, they keep you healthy and beautiful!

DOWNLOAD

Back when I was living in Japan, I used to go out to eat on a daily basis, and I wasn't yet in the habit of eating healthy. One day, as I helped myself to a large, savory meal at an Italian restaurant, a couple of older gentlemen sitting nearby began chatting with me. The attractive older man who sat next me informed me that he was celebrating his birthday that night. I'd guessed that perhaps he was turning 40 or so, but I was amazed when he said it was his 60th birthday! A senior citizen! Even by our famously youthful Japanese standards, he looked incredibly young for his years. I inspected him closely. He had beautiful, wrinkle-free skin, and a fine head of hair.

"Wow!" I'd exclaimed. "What's your secret to staying so young?"

With a big, boyish smile on his face, he told me:

"Being horny and happy!"

He then went on to speak lovingly of his wife; how they'd met, what a beauty she was, and how he adored her. They'd been married for decades, and God bless him, he was still absolutely in love with and horny for his wife of thirty years.

Be shameless. Shame is the opposite of being your true, authentic self. If you do something counter to your soul, you will wind up feeling ashamed. But if you are always honest with yourself and act accordingly, you will be without shame. Shamelessness amounts to happiness.

DOWNLOAD

12

CHAPTER TWO

relationship downloads

Ever wonder why you keep meeting what amounts to the same person in a different body over and over again—different faces, but still somebody with whom you've had the same kind of relationship? I always wondered about this, until I realized some patterns in my life that led me to this same person over and over again. The way I changed these patterns was by going spiritual. I realized that a relationship mirrors aspects of myself back to me. The way I react to situations can provide clues to my internal makeup; my complex emotional and spiritual circuits that cause me to respond in a certain way automatically because these "circuits" are programmed to be part of my subconscious mind.

You might think that your partner is someone that just turned up in your life by some kind of fate, or even randomly, and that he or she is just giving you particular experiences solely based on his or her personality or character. For example, we often describe our experiences with other people by saying "he is nice," "she is jealous and suspicious," "he is violent and possessive," and so on. We might say we feel "happy," "peaceful," "angry," "sad," or "anxious" when we engage in an actual relationship with another person. But have you ever thought about why you became attracted to this person in the first place?

Relationships are about how we interact with the Universe, our relationship to the whole, the self, God, and the macro level, otherwise known as the "big picture." We are part of the whole, and to be whole we need to realize that we *are* whole. The people who are closest to you, such as your lover, partner, boyfriend, girlfriend, or family members, can help with this process, as they hit our "subconscious buttons" which in turn bring out our hidden traits for us to experience *who we really are.*

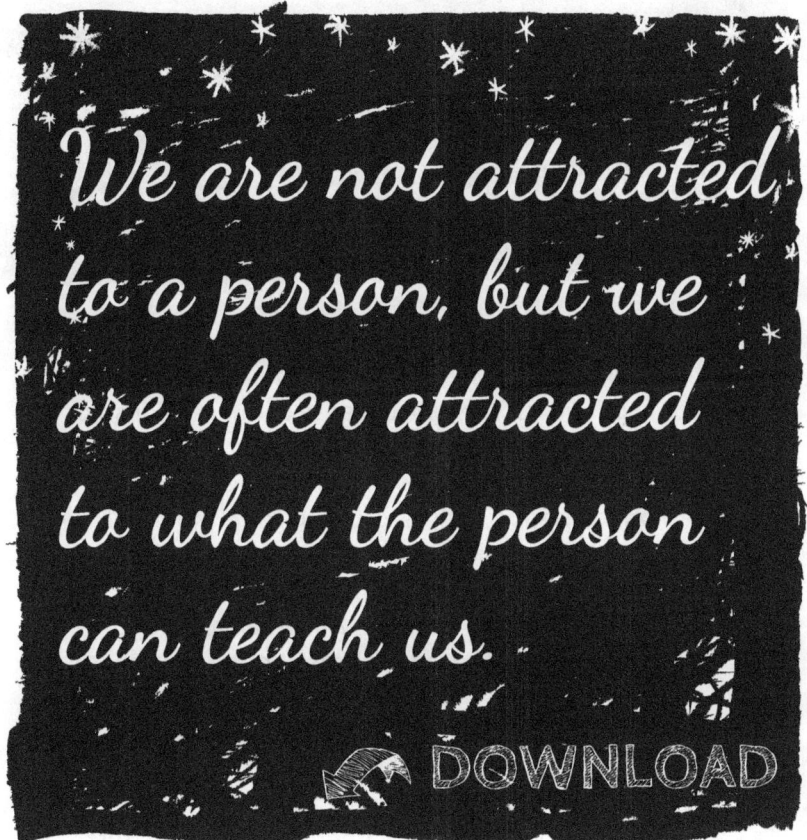

We are not attracted to a person, but we are often attracted to what the person can teach us.

DOWNLOAD

We don't consciously think this, but your *soul,* which has lived eons before your present life, knows what lessons you need to experience. So you are drawn to these *lessons* in a human form.

Sometimes our dark thoughts—especially if you have been feeling low for a long time—are not even coming from us. They are because of our relationships with others. And these feelings of anxiety and insecurity with another, when experienced over a prolonged period of time, cause us to be "hooked" upon by non-physical entities (i.e., paranormal monstrosities) that are floating around us. Think of these entities like bacteria, which centuries ago nobody believed existed. Well, believe it or not, these entities exist in our world, and they are energy parasites.

Let's suppose that, theoretically, these energetic parasites follow a kind of mathematical pattern. Just like the bacteria in our physical world, these energy parasites are attracted to low vibrations. When we physically get sick, it's due to our lowered immunity; this causes all kinds of parasites and bacteria that are otherwise harmless to destroy us by creating inflammation, tumors, and infections in our body. It's a mathematical certainty that this will happen.

So if you become gravely ill in a relationship, be aware. Your body is trying to tell you that somebody is triggering you to feel low. This is most probably the person you are in a relationship with. What can you do about it? How do you want to feel? What are the triggers? Can you heal the wounds that are causing you to react negatively?

Remember, nothing happens purely outside of us. Everything happens inside of us. How we feel may be triggered by another person, but we have those buttons inside of us. And you are the only person who has access to your emotional control panel. If the other person isn't treating you with kindness, think about *why* you are in a relationship with that person. Also, think about why this absence of kindness has been brought to your attention.

HAVE YOU EVER TREATED ANOTHER PERSON WITHOUT KINDNESS?

ARE YOU ALWAYS KIND TO OTHERS?

Beware of having dark and negative thoughts continuously for an extensive time, as they are like magnets to other dark and negative thoughts.

There are dark entities in this dimension that are attracted to dark thoughts and vibrations. They are etheric "parasites" that are otherwise harmless, just as physical parasites in one's body are harmless when the inner ecology is in balance. But when you exhibit negativity or surround yourself with negative people, these dark entities can thrive inside of you.

DOWNLOAD

When someone close to you in your life is bothering you, look within — what part of you feels bothered? The answer to your "troubled" relationship with another is inside of you.

DOWNLOAD

The "lesson" is not always clear in the middle of some tragedy. But as obscure as it might be, you will see the positive lesson once you are ready to learn from it.

Each person has his or her own lessons to learn in their own time. It isn't your responsibility to correct someone's wrongdoings. Defeat no one. Forgive the person and yourself over and over again, hundreds of times if you must, and move on for your own good.

We all have a strong desire to dwell on painful memories caused by those who did "wrong" to you. We may even seek justice at times, but there is something called the *"pain body,"* which is the ego part of you, that seeks more and more reasons for you to feel pain. In order to be released from this ego part of ourselves, we need to *forgive* both those in our lives that have done us wrong and ourselves.

DOWNLOAD

> When you really know yourself (i.e., the frighteningly animalistic side of yourself), acknowledge it and accept it. It is all part of you, just as your angelic light side is part of you. Once you do this, you can then feel compassion for others who show their animalistic side, as you are really no different than them.

Sometimes when we find ourselves in a deep hole, angels in human form appear and pull us out of it. Their task is very specific, and as soon as they are done with their task, they often leave our lives whether we like it or not.

Our life lessons are presented to us from the easiest level to the hardest. We can accept the lesson when it's easy, but often we get stubborn and don't learn from it. Then the next time that same lesson is presented, it's a bit harder to accept. If we keep ignoring it, eventually the lesson will come crushing down upon us, so to speak, and presented in its severest form, impossible to ignore. Which way you would prefer is entirely up to you. Either way, you will learn from it.

DOWNLOAD 23

No one defines us. Only you define yourself.

Once you stop lying to yourself, your life flows more easily. You will generally feel at ease with things, no matter the circumstances. You will also have a soul-lead life, rather than a life filled with regret.

DOWNLOAD 25

CHAPTER THREE

health

+

beauty

downloads

PEOPLE ALWAYS ASK ME, "HOW DO YOU LOOK SO YOUTHFUL? IS IT PURELY GENETIC?"

I WILL SHARE WITH YOU THE SECRET.

DOWNLOAD

Your mind holds the key to whether you grow old or remain youthful.

Before I realized this, I was not immune to aging. Not even my Japanese heritage or my forever youthful mother's DNA could completely protect me from the effects of too much stress. What helped me stay looking so young was my mind.

However, I didn't initially consider that the mind might hold the key to looking young and staying healthy. I figured it probably had something to do with what I was eating. So, having written a book on raw food nutrition and diet, I started to apply the knowledge I had towards healing my body. I digested therapeutic amounts of freshly squeezed wheat grass juice every day. It is nature's number one complete food, with numerous minerals, amino acids, enzymes, and vitamins. I also ate high quality, organic, plant-based proteins such as hemp seeds, rice, a variety of soaked nuts, green vegetables, and avocados. Despite this, my hair kept falling out, so I tried eating whole-foods full of B-vitamins and iron and taking high doses of probiotics as well. I even started eating parasite cleansing herbs, as I suspected parasites were afoot. I made sure I had enough hydration. All those things that once improved my health dramatically did not even make a dent. My hair continued to fall out. My face looked as bony as a skull. My energy kept dropping. I couldn't get out of bed no matter how many hours I slept. Every day I woke up exhausted. There is a medical condition called Chronic Fatigue Syndrome, and it seemed to me that I had developed this without even knowing it. My body was falling apart.

UNDOING THE TRAUMA

It seemed that no amount of food therapy could save my life. This got me thinking about where all illnesses come from. In the Japanese language, illness is written as 病気. "気" stands for "Ki," or "life force," and "病" literally means "illness." In Japan, there is a saying that goes, "All illnesses come from Ki." I believed this to be true, as I knew that my Ki was sick. Extreme stress in my life had shocked me, causing my body to break down at a rapid rate. I was eating healthy before my body started to die, so it wasn't due to an unhealthy junk food diet. I was healthy *before* the shock.

So how would I heal myself?

It was simple: do the opposite. *Un-shock* myself.

Reverse physical damage by "un-shocking" the Ki. DOWNLOAD

We all experience trauma to various degrees on a daily basis. It comes in the form of your work, your boss, your relationships, and your past. And when the trauma gets the best of us, we get wrinkles. We get sick. We start dying faster and faster.

Realizing this, I immediately started to attract information on how to un-shock my Ki. There is a term, "energy body," which addresses things like the

Chakra System, the Meridian System, the Aura, and the Causal Body. *Hmmm,* I thought to myself, *all these unfamiliar New Age concepts—what do they all mean for me?* Since they are part of the whole New Age ideology, should I even consider applying the ideas behind them to my dire situation?

Don't get fooled by the "New Age" label, as this energy body is very real! If it didn't exist, or was just some silly hocus pocus nonsense, then why do all these ancient healing systems as Yoga and Chinese acupuncture use it? And why did I attract this information to me after my dietary approach didn't work?

MY CHILDHOOD MASTER "KI" HEALER, MR. KAKIMOTO

If you want to know what an energy body, or the non-physical part of us—the mind, the soul, or the Ki—actually is, you can find hundreds of books on these subjects, or look them up online. As for me, I knew about Ki from my childhood Ki Master Healer, Mr. Yoshio Kakimoto, who was from the renowned Noguchi Seitai.

Noguchi Seitai is a Japanese non-profit, non-religious gymnastic organization founded by Haruchika Noguchi in the 1950s. Their aim is to educate the public to promote wellness and preventative health through self-healing exercises that consist of body movements and breath work, called "Katsugen." Noguchi, whom the organization is named after, had studied Rei-jutsu (energy healing work) under Chiwaki Matsumoto (considered by many to be the father of all Reiki, energy, and spiritual healing) in his teens, and became the pioneer of the Healing-Hands Technique and later Seitai Therapy, which is based on a very comprehensive holistic methodology. In layman's terms, it's a combination of acupuncture, osteopathy, yoga, and all things chiropractic. Seitai spread around the world under different names, such as Reiki, through different practitioners. Noguchi is said to have had only a few disciples in his life, and Mr. Kakimoto was one of them.

Mr. Kakimoto was gentle and handsome. He had a full head of gray hair and was full of nobility and poise. He visited our home in Tokyo every month to do healing sessions. It wasn't just me and my family that he healed; people from all over gathered at our house to receive treatments from him. He was extremely dedicated to serving people through his chosen work. I also remember him being a very humble soul who would always smile quite innocently whenever my mother served a piece of cake to him. The cake came from a local cake shop that used all natural ingredients. He loved all-natural sweets!

I also remember *hot wind* coming out of Mr. Kakimoto's hands during his healing sessions! He showed me how to produce a similar healing Ki with my hands using a technique called "Yu Ki." He was able to heal people just by holding his hands over their body. Every time he came over and helped my family and everyone else that attended the sessions, I became more and more convinced that what he did was *real*. I came to accept his abilities without question, and I eventually realized that I needed to start using what he taught me to heal my dying body. I decided to come up with some practical exercises based in the concepts of healing that Mr. Kakimoto showed me as a child.

MARTIAL ARTS FOR A SAGGING FACE

The ultimate facelift starts with your heart. It's the most natural method, and it does not require going under the knife. When you uplift your heart, you can uplift your facial muscles.

A sagging face looks sad, tired, and old. It represents how you've felt for too long. If you notice that your face is droopy, it's time you look deep into your soul, as it's trying to tell you that you're tired and unhappy!

DOWNLOAD
Quick heart up! Facelift exercise

 Stand in front of a mirror.
Imagine magnificent news being told to you, such as "You just won 10 million dollars!" or whatever else makes your heart dance.
Jump up and down in joy, while imagining your heart lifting upwards, screaming "Yay!" with a big smile on your face. Hold both your arms up in victory and jump into the sky. Visualize this in your mind.

☞ Do this for a minimum of three minutes.
☞ Repeat this exercise as often as you can during the day. The more often you do this, more potent the effect will be.

Sounds crazy? Yes, it certainly *looks* crazy. But believe me, it's a great remedy for depression, unhappiness, and negative feelings.

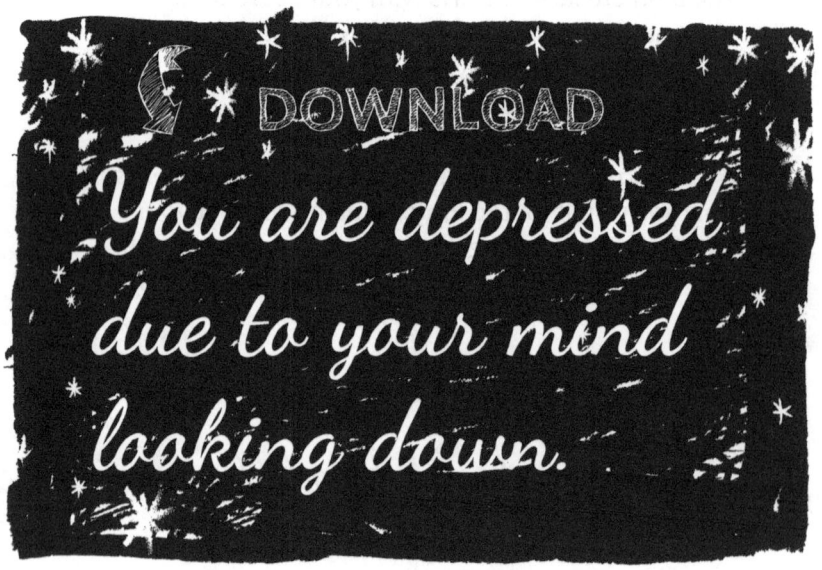

HOW TO DETOX YOUR ENERGY BODY

Here are the methodologies that I find to be the most effective:

MEDITATION
Earthing (connecting with nature using your bare feet, hands, and body)

FLOWER ESSENCE THERAPY
Working with Energy Healers, such as Channel Clearing Healers, Chakra Cleansing Healers, Seitai and Reiki Practitioners

CHAKRA CLEARING
Seitai (or Energy Healing, including Reiki)

MEDITATION

The point of doing meditation is that it produces a healing state. The deeply meditative state means that your brain is producing Theta waves, which are the brainwaves generated during the sleep state, *but without being asleep*. The key word here is being *awake* and having active Theta waves so that one can *consciously shift the subconscious mind*. Trauma is like a glitch trapped in the subconscious mind which needs to be released; otherwise, it will be stuck in there, producing a kind of malfunctioning "automatic pilot" situation in your brain. This in turn creates "blind spots" that you cannot see yourself, but others can see clearly. It's also why you can easily see solutions to everyone else's problems and not your own! Hence, meditation uses your *will* to affect the subconscious mind for healing.

If you are still learning how to meditate, I suggest that you use sound systems to help induce Theta brainwaves. Many online retailers sell "binaural" audio files that you can download onto your computer. You would need a good headphone set, as the sound needs to hit both your eardrums clearly so it can produce the meditative brainwave state inside you.

STEPS TO PRACTICE THETA WAVE MEDITATION

 Lay down comfortably on a bed or a floor and cover yourself with a blanket (if needed).

 Put on your headphones and play the sound for thirty minutes.

 During this time, imagine releasing all the energy garbage from your existence. This includes your resentment, anger, fears, sadness, and guilt.

 Send all the energy garbage back down to the core of the earth, and replace it with pure life force. Envision it as white light that comes into you from the bottom of your feet, moving all the way up to the top of your head and above your body, and finally filling up your entire existence.

You may cry or feel intense feelings from the meditation. If this happens, it's a very good sign. You are saying goodbye to the energy garbage.

Do this twice a day; once upon rising, and again before bed. Note: It's important that you do both the morning and evening meditations in order to maintain the healing effect.

HOW DO YOU KNOW IF YOU ARE PRODUCING THETA WAVES?

Theta waves are similar to dreams. If you start to see clear visions during meditation even though you are not sleeping, you are in the Theta state. You may see visions of things unrelated to the meditation, but they are just something being released or passing through your mind, so simply observe them. Try to remain unattached to the images and let them pass through your mind.

STRESS GETS STORED IN YOUR BRAIN!

It is said that stress actually gets stored in the hypothalamus. This accumulated stress creates the "fight or flight" syndrome, even when you're not conscious of having stress. Your brain keeps sending out distress signals to the rest of the body, which can cause malfunction of the organs, poor digestion, acidic pH, and a host of other chronic ailments. But with meditation, you can release all of this stored stress and receive the healing your body and soul need to survive.

"SEEING" MY GUARDIAN ANGEL, "BENKEI"

Sometimes, while meditating during my intense healing period (when I typically spent eight to ten hours a day meditating), I see visions.

I wanted to see my guardian angel, since I've always felt as if there is something circling my soul, protecting me, helping me learn my life lessons. During one particularly intense meditation session, I said, "Creator of the Universe, show me my guardian angels."

Suddenly I saw a name in Japanese writing: "弁慶"(in English, "Benkei").

I must admit that from living in America too long, not having paid much attention my own culture or the history of Japan, I didn't remember who this person was exactly. I did, however, remember that Benkei was someone from ancient times in Japan.

"Show me his face," I continued.

A picture of an ancient, armored Japanese warrior appeared in my mind.

Huh?

I went online and looked him up. It turns out that Benkei was a legendary warrior monk who lived over eight hundred years ago. There is a famous story about his death; he died standing, covered with arrows, at an entrance of the bridge leading to the castle of General Yoshitsune Minamoto while buying time for the general to commit *hara-kiri* (i.e., suicide) when defeat was imminent by their enemy's troop. It is said that Benkei was dead for quite some time before the enemy troops finally realized it. By the time they did, the enemy troops had been scared into believing that Benkei was immortal.

Benkei is known for his loyalty, wit, and strength. What puzzled me was that in my meditation, the name of my guardian angel appeared as Benkei, but the image I saw was Yoshitsune, as the armor I had seen belonged to him. Did this mean both Benkei and Yoshitsune were around me? Or did Benkei want to show his master's image instead of himself? I have no idea. I didn't ask for either of them to appear in my meditation. So, what did that mean?

Still…

"Cool!" I thought to myself. What more could I have asked for than Benkei as my protector? It seemed logical, being that I have survived so much in my life that should've probably killed me.

Another thought struck me: is it possible that I was Yoshitsune? I've always thought there is a strong Samurai General in me. I dismissed this as just some very grand speculation on my part, but who knows? Anything is possible…

MORE VISIONS, AND INTRODUCING TREE HUGGNG FOR DETOXING MY ENERGY BODY

During meditation one day, I saw a vision of an entity that most people would probably call an "elf." I guess the only comparison I can make would be to the elves in *Lord of the Rings*. And no, I wasn't hallucinating or using drugs!

He was standing in the doorway, looking at me. After a while, he pointed outside and said to me, "Go out to the yard and hug that tree. It can heal you."

I looked at the tree he was talking about. It was an old pine tree lying horizontally just above the ground. It wasn't dead, but it looked as if it was, and it made a perfect bench for me to sit on. So I went outside and stood by the tree, and it immediately invited me to use it to heal myself. It was as if I heard a voice saying "Hug me" in my mind. So… I hugged the tree!

There I was: an official TREE HUGGING HIPPIE! I didn't quite understand how this would heal me at first, but soon, a feeling welled up inside me, like being *pulled down to the ground*. Or in other words, I felt *grounded*. I also felt lighter, as if some kind of huge heaviness in my chest had been lifted.

Intrigued by the experience, I did some research on the pine tree as an alternative remedy for trauma. What I found was that in Flower Essence Therapy, which is used to heal deep energetic trauma and subconscious programming, pine is a remedy for self-blame and guilt.

Right away, I realized that the "poison" eating me up from within was guilt. I had a lot of self-blame and guilt in my life. I had failed at a relationship that became abusive in the end. I didn't know how to deal with being abused in a relationship, so it seemed logical somehow that I wanted to "punish myself" by feeling guilty for what had happened. I felt so guilty at times that I felt like perishing! Even after I had left the relationship and there wasn't anyone around to hurt me, I still felt like I had to blame myself for everything that went wrong in my life. I was on auto-pilot with blame!

Practice forgiveness first and foremost on yourself. If you don't know how to forgive yourself, you don't know how to forgive anything.

TREE HUGGING THERAPY

- Pick a tree of your choice (preferably one someplace where you can have total privacy).
- Approach it with *appreciation* (you can say thank you for helping, either in your mind or out loud).
- Hug the tree and visualize your feelings of pain and suffering getting sucked into the tree.
- You may cry, or scream, or moan. Whatever comes out must come out.
- Visualize the tree recycling that poison back into the earth, and after it's purified, visualize the tree sending you back a more pure life force.
- When you feel lighter, you're finished!

Alternatively, you can practice breathing exercises of your choice, such as Pranayama in Yoga, Qi Gong, or Tai Chi while in front of the tree. Do any of these exercises to help throw the unwanted energy into the tree. And always remember to thank the tree for its help.

OTHER TYPES OF EARTHING STYLE HEALING EXERCISES

- Walking barefoot on the grass or in nature.
- Swimming in natural waters, such as lakes and the ocean.
- Bathing in natural hot springs.
- Soaking in natural mud or clay.
- Smelling flowers.

FLOWER ESSENCE THERAPY

Similar to homeopathy, which contains only the minimum amount of medicinal ingredients in distilled water necessary to stimulate the body's natural healing power and heal specific *physical* ailments, Flower Essences are liquids containing only the *energy* of the flowers or plants that are used for healing specific emotions or traumas, energetic blockage, or even for promoting positive emotions such as optimism, confidence, forgiveness, and compassion. It's said that each flower has its own intelligence and vibration which, when ingested by humans or animals, affects and corrects the emotional and spiritual imbalances in whomever or whatever ingests it.

Dr. Edward Bach in England, a highly regarded homeopath, invented Flower Essences Therapy in the 1930s. Since then, his brand, Bach Flower Remedy Essences, has been distributed around the world. These days, there are many flower essence companies around the world producing extraordinarily unique essences, including those made from gemstones and from environments like the North Pole and the ocean. Each essence is supposed to contain the "vibration" of its environment. Neat, isn't it?

While meditation requires a great deal of concentration and time to produce its karma-melting effects (or as I like to think of it, as an energy detox), Flower Essences are that extra "push" into positivity that you can use at any time. When you are too busy, you may stop meditating, but Flower Essences are like "liquid meditation" that you can spray under your tongue several times a day. They can keep melting away all your energy garbage while you go about your business.

In fact, I love this concept so much that I created a two ounce spray bottle of Flower Essence liquid to use whenever my soul needs a boost. For my spray bottle concoction, I mix drops of "mother stock" (i.e., undiluted original liquid that contains the energy of the plant) flower essences from New Zealand (which I found online while searching for flower essences for Post Traumatic Syndrome) with diluted water and organic brandy to avoid molding. I sprayed it under my tongue every hour or so throughout the day; this was, by the way, a *lot* more than a normal dose. Typically one would take it three or four times daily, but it's okay to use more, as the essences are completely non-toxic. Just remember: the potency is increased by the *frequency* of the ingestion, not by the quantity.

FLOWER ESSENCES WORK WITH ANIMALS TOO

As I studied Flower Essence Therapy, I was living in a place that had a beautiful young cat. However, this cat was having a difficult time, losing teeth despite its very young age. It seemed that the cat didn't have very strong DNA, and it ate processed dry cat food exclusively. I felt that the cat needed some healing, so I started feeding the cat raw meat and raw milk. The cat initially showed no interest in what I offered! This poor cat was also weak, and afraid of everything in its environment. I decided to give it a flower essence which was supposed to bring out its innate qualities. Immediately after I did this, the cat started to sleep a lot. And I mean a *lot*—it slept two or three days in a row! When the cat woke up, it decided to go hunting; about two weeks later, it came home with something hanging out of its mouth. There was a tiny mouse between its jaws! Amazingly, this was the first time that the cat had ever gone hunting! I watched as the cat strutted inside the apartment and proudly dropped its prey right in front of me.

I was in awe at witnessing its transformation. I wasn't so much in awe, however, when the cat devoured the mouse and left only its head on the floor, which I of course had to clean up.

HOW TO TAKE FLOWER ESSENCES

- Choose the essences based on whatever ailment or condition you're experiencing.
- Prepare a dark glass bottle with a spray top. Size should be either one or two ounces. Pour one part organic brandy (or vinegar if you want a non-alcoholic version) into the bottle. Add three parts water.
- Add four to seven drops of each essence, depending on the brand you choose. Follow the manufacturer's instructions as to exactly how many drops you should use.
- Spray into your mouth sublingually three or four times a day. If the condition is severe, you may

choose to take it as often as every hour or half an hour.

NOTE: You might experience an energy "detoxifying" healing crisis, similar to the physical detox from fasting or juice fasting. That is, you might start feeling that you're attempting to heal *too much*. For example, if you're attempting to heal anger and promote forgiveness, you could potentially release explosive anger! This happened to me, and when I realized it, I had to cut the dosage by half. I felt sorry for those around me! I hadn't realized it, but I had been taking the essence as often as every hour. This had proved to be entirely too much for me to handle. So, if the detoxification of your negative feelings becomes too much to handle, simply reduce the dosage or stop for a day and start again the next day at a lower dosage.

Choosing the right flower essences can take some research on your part. I've used multiple brands, including Australian Bush Flower Essences, Alaskan Essences, and FES. The most unique and cutting-edge essence I used was a brand called New Millennium Flower Essences, created by New Zealander Peter Archer. His flower essences are named after the condition they address. Some of these include:

- Complex Pattern Unraveller
- Compulsive Dysfunctional Pattern
- Subconscious Hooks
- Intuition and Lessons Integration
- Feelings Validator
- Shadow-Self and Ego

I actually still use New Millennium Flower Essences extensively. They have essences for Post-Traumatic Stress Syndrome, and also for getting rid of the "dark entities" in my life. I stopped having dark thoughts after using Flower Essences, so it worked for me. Is this hocus-pocus? I'll let you be the judge. Just make sure you choose the *right* essences, or they won't work.

WORKING WITH ENERGY HEALERS

Working with energy healers is one of the most powerful ways to detox your energy body. There are many types of energy healers that can help you. Meridian Channel Clearing healers, Reiki healers, and Seitai practitioners can all help get rid of your energy garbage.

One healer I discovered uses a unique method that addresses the soul of a seriously ill person. This individual, Dr. Sha, has a healing center in Canada that attracts people from all around the world. I watched his videos and was in total agreement with his methods; he approaches energy healing like it's the Martial Arts of healing. He believes he pierces into the precise location of energy blockage or trauma and dissolves it, so that the life force of the person can flow properly and the illness can disappear.

In fact, the fastest healing I have ever learned came from an energy healing. I watched as a cancerous tumor was dissolved with the help of two energy healers in just three minutes! Now that is *fast!*

CHAPTER FOUR

*love +
romance
+ sex
downloads*

I HAVE LEARNED THAT MONEY AND MATERIAL POSSESSIONS ALONE COULD NOT MAKE ME HAPPY. THAT WAS THE "EMPTINESS" I FELT IN NEW YORK BACK IN EARLY 2000.

Love has always been the number one priority for me. Without love, nothing else matters. That was why when I had problems in a relationship, my life fell apart. It was also because I didn't know how to tame the wild horse that is my mind. You see, the mind, which connects our physical body to our non-physical self, can't be seen with your eyeballs, the same way that ideas are non-physical. Yet the mind is the generator of ideas, which then materialize into physical things. And this powerful "idea generator" is like a beastly stallion; it's strong, and has the ability to manifest physical reality, but if it's not tame, the mind gets totally out of control. The reason is because it's powered by feelings, which are like the enzymes of nature. Enzymes are the catalysts in all biological activities. Without them, your body can't utilize nutrients from food. Matters of love to me are like life-or-death situations because they directly connect to my soul—at least until I realized something about true love and loneliness.

"Are men from some regions more commitment-phobic than men from other regions?"

I read an article written by woman who was ready to move out of San Francisco after living there for ten years. This was because she found that "men in San

Francisco are commitment-phobic and not into things like family, love, and commitment."

I thought about my own relationship history. I had dated two men in the past twelve months in San Francisco. Both disappeared after a few dates. But I also met more men who wanted *my* commitment for a relationship, and I just wasn't attracted to them. So, I couldn't agree with the generalization that *all* men in San Francisco won't commit to a serious relationship.

On the other hand, men have told me they can't meet any women in San Francisco. But when I hear this, I always think the same thing: both women *and* men in San Francisco must be lonely. I certainly could say I was, to a certain degree.

When you feel the void that loneliness brings, it means that something is lacking inside of you. And it's almost certain that you'll focus on what's lacking too.

What is the *essence* of loneliness? I believe it's a *void*. And the reason why you have the void is because you're paying full attention to it. Look at a child who is so full of ideas to keep her occupied. She's not looking to fill a void, and so she's happy.

It's really that simple.

When you start to feel depressed or think negative thoughts, say to yourself: "I am looking for reasons to feel happy." This commands your mind to find reasons to be happy instantly.

Forget that you are single, unless of course being single is what you want. Instead, focus on the *essence* of what a wonderful fulfilling relationship can offer you. How would you feel in such a relationship?

Passionate? I would.

Don't get me wrong; I've been through a "forget passion" phase. I felt that passion was over-rated. What I felt I needed was security. I then fell for someone who offered me security but no passion, but this didn't make me happy. I realized that we are part animal and part spirit, which means we're supposed to find a mate that is a perfect match on all levels—mind, body, and soul. This made me consider the possibility that we *all* need passion to be happy. So ask yourself: do you have passion? In *anything*?

Fulfillment is the absence of a *void*. You can't have a void-based relationship and feel truly fulfilled at the same time.

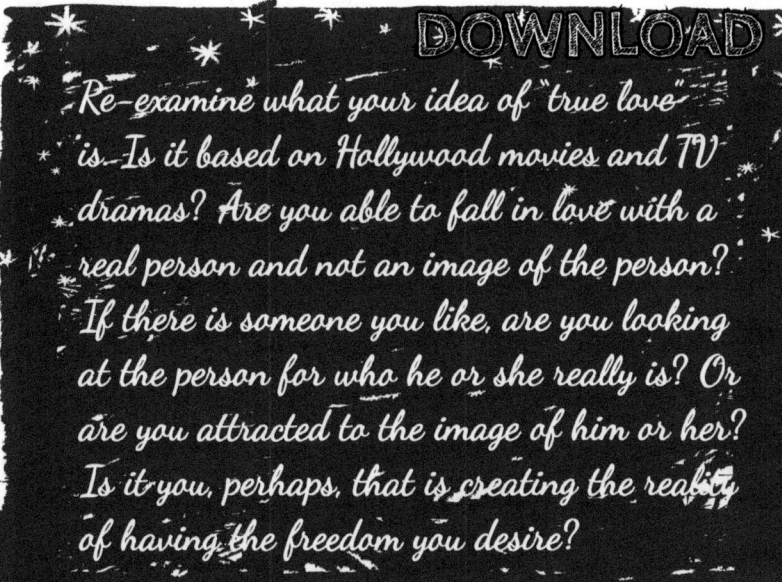

DOWNLOAD

Re-examine what your idea of "true love" is. Is it based on Hollywood movies and TV dramas? Are you able to fall in love with a real person and not an image of the person? If there is someone you like, are you looking at the person for who he or she really is? Or are you attracted to the image of him or her? Is it you, perhaps, that is creating the reality of having the freedom you desire?

**ARE YOU COMMITTED TO YOUR WELL-BEING
AND HAPPINESS?**

Be happy. The end goal is happiness. Don't be lazy. Wake up! You are the only person who can make your happiness a reality. Be the creator of your happiness, just like a child.

DOWNLOAD

ON SELF-ESTEEM

A lot of us have low self-esteem that often stems from childhood and not accepting who we are. As a result, we attract a mate who mirrors what we are like inside of ourselves.

If we are not in love with ourselves—and by this I don't mean narcissism, but being comfortable with whom we are, flaws and all—then we create disharmony within ourselves. This discord then manifests as disharmony in our relationships.

I feel we all want to be accepted and loved for who we are. But can you give that same love and acceptance to another?
When you truly love yourself, you know what you deserve, and if someone approaches you who can't accept and love you as you are, as a simple human being who wants to love and be loved, then you need to let this person go back into the Universe. You can always trust that the Universe will send somebody else to love and who will love you, too.

DOWNLOAD

When the Universe sends us a "lemon," send it back. If you accept a lemon due to insecurity, you are selling yourself short, and you won't get what you really want. Don't settle for less. You deserve true love.

WHAT IS A "SOUL MATE"?

A soul mate, in the traditional sense, is often called your "other half". It's someone you meet and just know she or he is "the *one*." According to soul mate experts, there are several types of soul mates.

TWIN FLAME

This person is called your "other half," because he or she is the other half of the same soul that had split into two when it first came into existence eons ago. Very few people will ever meet their twin flame. Along with this, it's said that a relationship with a twin flame is very difficult, because they are an exact mirror of you. This can cause intense drama in the relationship. Often twin flames can't stay together due to the intensity of the energy. But it's also said that when twin flames work out their difficulties, the relationship can blossom.

KARMIC MATES

Simply put, karmic mates are people who you've shared some times together in your past lives. They come into your life to teach you lessons or to finish some unfinished business from a previous life. The relationship is often traumatic and painful, and ends once the lesson is learned.

ROMANTIC SOUL MATES AND FAMILY OR FRIEND SOUL MATES

Your true love can be called a romantic soul mate, whereas friend or family soul mates can be identified by their sense of ease, familiarity, and comfort.
Some of my close friends are definitely my soul mates. These are the people in my life who unconditionally love me and know me. From the moment we met, I never have had to explain a lot about myself to them; they just seemed to "get" me, and have been there for me throughout the highs and lows of my life. This feeling is mutual, believe me. There are no hidden agendas between us.

I met one of my friend soul mates, Christian, when I went back to Tokyo. There was an instant click between us, and being the charming, attractive, and very intelligent fashion model that he was, he had a lot of friends; I, staying busy as a published book author, somehow still ended up spending most of my time with him. We spent much of our time together in Tokyo hunting and searching for dark chocolates that we both loved. Our time together was always positive, fun, and light-hearted. We never fought either, mostly because between us, we had nothing to fight about. There was a sense of love and respect for each other right from the start, and it's still there today between us.

When you meet someone with whom you have a soul connection, you can identify that connection by listening to your soul to answer the question, "Have I known you from before?"

I used to get urinary tract infections only when I made love to men who I felt uncomfortable with or unsafe with. This feeling was at the deepest level, like some kind of an animal or spiritual instinct. It happened a lot with my ex-boyfriend, who was violent. Because of this, I now trust my body's attempt to communicate with me. Urinary tract infections were my body's way of preventing me from engaging in physical intimacy with dangerous individuals. I took this as a spiritual message and trusted it. And why not? You need to trust your sexual partners 100%. Sex is an act of sacred unity between male and female. Since you exchange DNA with your partner and a piece of their soul in physical form enters you, *becomes a part of you*, it's nothing to be taken lightly.

We are part animal and part spirit. Everything is spiritual, for nothing could come into existence without the spirit, but without the flesh, we can't exist.

You will know real love when it happens. It doesn't come with stress or complications. There will perhaps be difficulties in your relationship, but you will never have to compromise your self-respect or untwine your moral fiber for the person you love.

The love of your life will provoke the strongest animalistic desire in you, as well as provide you with comfort, stability, and supportive energy. Without the animalistic part, we can't make love as Yin and Yang energies merging to be one. Remember, we live in a material dimension—everything is experienced physically, even dreams, deep mediation, and astral travel. These things are all experienced through your senses. So embrace the animalistic aspect of yourself as well as the non-physical. We are without doubt multi-dimensional beings.

DOWNLOAD

Your true soul mate is yourself. You don't need to go anywhere to find "the one." The one is you. Be at ease knowing that you are with the one already.

 **DOWNLOAD**

CHAPTER FIVE

laws of the universe downloads

WHAT IS REALITY?

Some would say that reality is a 3-D world, dense with material things. I prefer to look at reality as the place where your soul collects memories and learns. It's where your soul takes notes and records every experience.

The dream world, on the other hand, is the not-yet-materialized reality. Both versions of reality have 3-D experiences; one is felt with your *materialized* body, the other is felt with your *non-materialized* body. Both worlds intertwine with each other, just like your body, mind, and soul intertwine with each other.

DREAM WORLD VS. REAL WORLD

Since I was a child, I've always had the ability to remember my dreams without writing them down. I would vividly remember names, people, and places. Sometimes I would even be aware that I was dreaming.

I use dreams to understand the universe, what is going on in the present, and what is yet to come in my life.

Dreams have helped me understand the world around me, particularly the world of men. One day, right around the time I was moving on from a relationship with a commitment-phobic man, I asked myself, "I want to understand men better—what is it like to be a man?"

That night, I was a man in my dream. Now, I've had dreams about aliens, sorcerers, parallel universes, and different dimensions, but this one was a first!

I looked at myself. I had a man's body. I was a good-looking and fit; I was what some might call a "tall, dark, and handsome" kind of man. The same kind of man I would be attracted to.
What's more, I was, um, being intimate with a dark-skinned woman! Now, I don't think I would have this kind of fantasy when I am awake, but as a man, I knew what I wanted and felt!

I woke up and said to myself, "Holy heaven…"

I suddenly understood how a man's mind works, as I perceived the woman as being a soft, feminine, receptive Yin that responded to my male, Yang energy, and together we were like tides of the ocean. Ying and Yang. It was really beautiful.

Another time, I asked myself, *"What happens after death?"*

That night, believe it or not, I died in my dream! I was a female soldier, fighting in a war zone, and got blasted by missiles. I saw myself die in slow motion. I felt unbearable stress inside my body, and then everything went dark. Right after this happened, I found myself outside of my body. I was just a spirit. But I wasn't sad about this; on the contrary, I was both happy and excited to finally understand what happens when you die! I also wanted to tell my friends and family that death was *not painful*! It was

merely a transfer from one place to another.
I still existed.

Another thing that was interesting about my dream death: when I looked at my "ghost body," I noticed that I retained the image of the person I was when I died. I was wearing the pajamas I used to wear. Then I remembered how I died and suddenly, my pajamas got bloody. I thought to myself, *Uh oh, this doesn't look too pretty. Let's change it*. So I changed the image of my ghost body to a healthy state. I was going to visit my friends and family, and didn't want to scare them!

I learned that a ghost body retains the image of the person when they pass, and they can also change this image at will.

Before I went any further as a ghost, I wanted to visit my loved ones. To do this, all I had to do was think of my loved ones and I was right in front of them. *Instantly*.

I tried telling them that I was *totally fine,* and that death was nothing to be afraid of. Unfortunately, no matter how hard I tried to communicate with them, they couldn't see me or hear me.

LUCID DREAMING

One day, I asked myself, *Is the conscious world the real world, or is the dream world what's actually real?* We perceive the world and its reality through our senses. Without our brain, which perceives colors, textures, tastes, smells, and sounds, can we really experience what is known as reality? Is reality happening purely outside of us, or is it *us*, the observers of reality, manufacturing it all? Could it be possible that what we perceive as reality is just one *big dream*?

That night, I experienced a lucid dream. I was totally aware I was in my dream world, and immediately wanted to test out how this world was different from the real world. I first tested my sense of touch. In the dream, I was in front of a fence covered with flowers. I pluck one of the flowers and could feel its soft texture between my fingers. I then carefully plucked the petals, one by one. They felt exactly the same as petals on flowers in the real world.

Next, I pushed myself against the fence, applying my body weight as I would in the real world. The fence was resilient. Consequently, the cold metallic mesh cut into my hands as I bounced backwards from the fence. I then smelled my hand, which reeked of metal. *Hmm… just like in the real world*, I thought to myself.

For the final part of the dream, I ventured into a house and touched everything: tables, chairs, the walls, everything. I probably would have looked silly if anyone had seen me do this, but once again, every surface I felt inside the house felt exactly the same as they would in the real world!

You can experience everything in the dream world just as you would in the real world.

The dream world represents the *potential truth* of this Universe, i.e., that *all things are possible*. You can fly, change your appearance, shape-shift, warp or teleport, talk to aliens or animals, watch animals talk to each other, and so on.

It seems that in the dream world, we can make things that are thought to be "impossible" possible. In other words, we *dream up* reality.

DOWNLOAD

The 3D world is a reality created in the minds of humans.

The reality world that we live in is three-dimensional. It is also filled with duality, such as black and white, right and wrong, light and shadow, good and bad, full and empty. But how do we perceive this 3-D world with our eyes, mind, and soul? Just like watching a movie using 3-D glasses, what is the "equivalent" of the two different images that come through us and create the final 3-D perception in our mind?

One is the *universal consciousness*, which can be called your "oneness".

The other is *your consciousness*, which is your "*creative force*" and "*desire.*"

This is why we as humans experience life as a 3-D reality. As long as we possess the creative force, there will always be duality, and vice versa. And the Universe is an *all-inclusive oneness* that contains humans with *desires* that are waiting to be manifested in reality. At the end of the day, we are all *creators*.

DOWNLOAD

The Universe contains the three-dimensional world as well as other dimensional worlds. It's only in the third dimension that things need to be black and white.

In our black and white human minds, we can only perceive the *oneness* as an abstract idea. Human minds intertwine with the *universal mind*, but humans can't experience the *oneness* in materialized reality. There is no 3-D picture that can describe the experience of *oneness*.

Time does not have a straight, chronological progressive order, as in 1, 2, 3, 4, and so on. It's a concept created by humans to help organize what we do in reality, but it's possible to not to fall within the parameters of time; the creator of all things is limitless, and we are all part of this limitlessness.

DOWNLOAD

In this *space* called *time*, changes take place that consist of either new to old or life to death. And no amount of time is set in stone for all of humanity to follow. Just think about the average human lifespan. It's generally accepted that the average human lifespan is anywhere from sixty to eighty years old, but how long a person actually lives isn't married to this timeline, is it? What's important to consider is that changes don't have to be *within a perceived time-space*. It's up to the creator of *your* reality: *you*.

So if you wish to "turn back the clock" in your life, set yourself free from the idea that time is a chronological straight line. You have the power to change *your form* as you wish.

DOWNLOAD

Time is an illusion. Eternal space is what we have. You have all the time in the world to be, do, and have anything you wish.

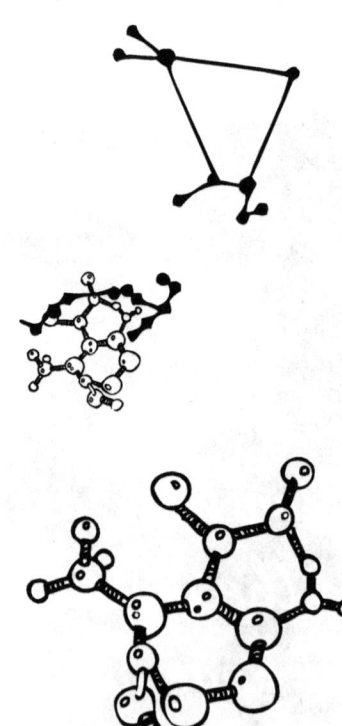

CHAPTER SIX

*manifesting
abundance
downloads*

Words and phrases like "manifesting," "the law of attraction," and "how to manifest xxx" have become quite popular these days, thanks to books like *The Secret* by Rhonda Byrne and *The Law of Attraction* by Esther & Jerry Hicks. In fact, there are actually dozens books on these topics.

I have noticed since becoming more aware of my spiritual side and getting in touch with my true nature, that money and material abundance become less of a concern, which caused them to become less present in my life.

As I discussed in my previous chapter on the Universe, what we focus on will make up the bulk of what's to be found in our lives. So when we focus on having money and material abundance, there will be more of these things in our lives.

What we all want is happiness, not money or material possessions, but the *lack* of money and material possessions may cause us to feel unhappy. But even if you are successful and have lots of money, that doesn't mean you will be happy either—just like I wasn't happy back in early 2000. So how do we have an abundance of money and possessions and still be happy at the same time? Or should we all just aim to be poor and forget about ever attaining any kind of wealth or material goods in this world?

This takes a little bit of digging into your true nature. You need to become aware of what it is that you really *love* doing, being, and feeling. When you find out what it is you love doing, you might have to take a detour in your career. Now, I know that we all need to have an income of some kind. We all have rent to pay, unless you are of course lucky to live at your family's home or someplace else rent-free.

One of the key things that keeps us from living the life we want is *fear;* fear of the unknown, of losing control, being broke, getting no respect from anyone, disapproval, not fitting in—the list goes on and on. Yet fear is a part of us, whether we like it or not, and it can help keep us from getting hurt, both physically and emotionally. We are born equipped with the fear mechanism so we can increase our chances of living longer. But fear shouldn't dictate us. Our primal force should be *love*, which is the opposite of fear. *Love* inspires us to follow our dreams and our desires despite the consequences. Love is truly something that enchants us.

It's important then that we pursue what we love while creating money and material abundance. This is the path to contentment. And above all, you should pursue what you love like it's your last day on earth and your last life to live in the Universe.

If you live your life as if it is your last one, you will do everything possible to achieve happiness. You will be shameless. You will be authentic. You will try to succeed no matter what. So take a chance on going after what you love! It's never too late.

Keep becoming aware of your focus. When you focus on your creative force with razor-sharp precision, you will manifest and materialize what you desire into your 3D reality.

At some point in our lives, most of us have encountered a situation where we are desperate for money. I have experienced a situation where it felt as if I had jumped out of an airplane 5,000 feet from the ground without a parachute—and had no clue what to do next! There was no cushion, no backup plan. In that kind of extreme situation, no amount of panicking will do you any good. All I could do was turn to the Universe. Since this is where *all* things come from, I believed this was a viable choice in "manifesting" or attracting money quickly.

It worked!

I was able to find the funds I needed just in time! Are you wondering exactly how I did this? Well, since it won't hurt you to try, sit quietly in your bedroom and practice the following:

Think of a specific amount of money you would like to receive, then enter into a Theta state meditation. Visualize and feel yourself not only possessing the desired money, but visualize yourself spending that money. Visualize it exactly, e.g., spending it on the rent, mortgage, car insurance, cell phone bill, and any other necessary things you need to pay for or buy. Do all of this with cheer and joy. This will allow you to get away from the "I don't-have-money" energies, like worry and panic, which actually attract more situations where you will not have the money you need. Lastly, remember to thank the creator, as well as whomever of wherever the money comes from once it manifests in your life.

 DOWNLOAD

**USE YOUR DREAMS TO EMPOWER YOU:
SYMBOLS IN YOUR DREAMS**

Not long ago, I had a dream with several big turtles. I was in a large bathtub with them, and was freaking out about it, since I thought they were dirty and carried parasites. I really wanted to get out of the tub, but somehow I couldn't move. Suddenly, one of the turtles started melting in the hot water in the tub, and I found myself bathing in the flesh of the turtle!

I had another dream about turtles. I was in a house, hanging out with them, watching as they gathered around me. I knew they weren't going to hurt me but, nevertheless I was feeling a bit uneasy. Then I woke up. It wasn't really a bad dream per se, but it was an *odd* dream for sure.

Most dream interpreters believe that turtles are symbols of good luck, vitality, and success. But I freaked out over the turtle dreams I was having. The mixed messages about what the turtles actually meant left me confused and wondering what would happen next in my life.

The answer to what the turtles meant came to me soon enough. I was contacted by a Japanese television production company (to this day, I still don't know how they got my email address) about appearing on a regionally televised show in Japan! I told them yes, but initially thought they wanted me to be a minor guest. I had no idea what was in store for me.

When I went onto the show's website to do research about the program, I learned that my part would be a major part, not a bit part as I originally imagined. Then I started to feel a sense of panic creeping up in me. I started to freak out—they picked me to be one of the hosts of an upcoming show! I wasn't used to this kind of big part on a TV show. Sure, I've been on TV in Japan before, but only for about two minutes.

Can you see the connection with the turtle dreams I had?

The turtles gave me unusual feelings, and even provoked fears inside of me. But they also indicated to me that a business opportunity was coming my way, and possibly money as well.

Along with this, I came across another interpretation of what turtles mean in dreams. It is said that turtles indicate the need to take a bold step in life, in order to prove myself worthy of a once-in-a-lifetime opportunity.

As it turned out, my appearance on the TV show was a huge success.

Pay attention to uncomfortable feelings. Are they from insecurity or fear, or is it your gut feeling telling you that something isn't right for you? These are totally different uncomfortable feelings. If it's insecurity or fear, go for it. Don't let fear stop you.

DOWNLOAD

DEALING WITH INSECURITY AND SELF-DOUBT

It would be inauthentic of me to say I can always overcome the insecurity and self-doubt in my life. The key is to find a balance between insecurity and confidence. Too much insecurity and self-doubt is not good for you, and too much confidence leads to *arrogance*, which isn't helpful either.

You need to learn to be patient, receptive, and bold. You need to learn how to reflect and recuperate, to be worldly, and to come home and find that the blueprint of happiness has always been there in your life.

No matter what you do, follow your soul. Trust that you are doing *exactly* what you are supposed to be doing, even if the situation doesn't seem like the Universe is supporting you.

CONCLUSION

I hope that the wisdom in this book has touched some people. I am no Jesus, or a master of any kind; quite the contrary, I'm just like you—an ordinary person who is discovering life. I feel that one of my missions in life is to share the downloads that the Universe has given me. I also believe that once we reach a certain awareness about who we are, there is no turning back. Just like in the movie The Matrix, *once you take the red pill, you can't return to your old life, no matter how hard you try. This is what happened to me. I'm sure there will be a lot more downloads to come. The Universe keeps evolving, and I keep evolving with it. I will keep documenting these downloads and share them with the world.*

ABOUT THE AUTHOR

Mihoko Sekido hails from Tokyo, she came to America in 1998 to work in the IT industry in New York. She has always been involved in pioneering work, from being a member of the beginning stage of the very first classified paper in Japan, to inventing gluten free muffins with "Mihoko's Magnificent Muffins".
Her avid interest in nutrition and alternative healing methodologies led her to write the first book on raw food diets

that was ever published in Japan (Hajimetemiyo Raw Food Seikatsu, published by Kashiwa Shobo, 2005). Consequently, this book is credited by many to have started a raw food movement in the country. In addition to her publishing endeavors, Mihoko has also written numerous articles in Japanese publications, worked with celebrities, and appeared on various television shows in Japan. She currently lives in San Francisco.

www.ingramcontent.com/pod-product-compliance
Lightning Source LLC
Chambersburg PA
CBHW071302040426
42444CB00009B/1829